W9-CHT-819

Amazing Animals
Lions

Jacqueline Dineen

WEIGL PUBLISHERS INC.

Published by Weigl Publishers Inc.
350 5th Avenue, Suite 3304, PMB 6G
New York, NY 10118-0069

Amazing Animals series ©2010
WEIGL PUBLISHERS INC. www.weigl.com
All rights reserved. No part of this
publication may be reproduced, stored
in a retrieval system, or transmitted in
any form or by any means, electronic,
mechanical, photocopying, recording,
or otherwise, without the prior written
permission of the publisher.

Library of Congress Cataloging-in-
Publication Data

Library of Congress Cataloging-in-
Publication Data available upon request.
Fax 1-866-44-WEIGL for the attention of
the Publishing Records department.

ISBN 978-1-60596-150-7 (hard cover)
ISBN 978-1-60596-151-4 (soft cover)

Editor
Heather Kissock
Design and Layout
Terry Paulhus, Kathryn Livingstone

Photograph Credits
Every reasonable effort has been
made to trace ownership and to obtain
permission to reprint copyright material.
The publishers would be pleased to have
any errors or omissions brought to their
attention so that they may be corrected
in subsequent printings.

Weigl acknowledges Getty Images as its
primary image supplier for this title.

Printed in China
1 2 3 4 5 6 7 8 9 0   13 12 11 10 09

About This Book

This book tells you all about
lions. Find out where they live
and what they eat. Discover
how you can help to protect
them. You can also read about
them in myths and legends
from around the world.

Words in **bold** are explained in the
Words to Know section at the back
of the book.

Useful Websites

Addresses in this book
take you to the home
pages of websites that
have information
about lions.

All of the Internet URLs given in
the book were valid at the time
of publication. However, due to
the dynamic nature of the Internet,
some addresses may have changed,
or sites may have ceased to exist
since publication. While the author
and publisher regret any
inconvenience this may cause
readers, no responsibility for any
such changes can be accepted by
either the author or the publisher.

Contents

Meet the Lion

A lion is a large animal with four strong legs and sharp teeth. A female lion is called a lioness. Lions are **mammals**, which are animals that feed their babies milk and have hair or fur on their bodies.

Lions belong to the same family as pet cats, but a person could not keep a mighty lion as a pet. It is one of the fiercest **predators** on Earth.

▼ Lions are known as the "kings of beasts" because they are very strong.

Useful Websites

www.thebigzoo.com/ Animals/African__Lion.asp

Find information about lions by visiting this website.

Lion Facts

- Lions are the second-largest cats in the world. Tigers are the largest of all cats.

- A lion's claws can be three inches (7.6 centimeters) long.

- A lion can jump as far as 30 feet (9 meters).

▲ A lioness, or female lion, is smaller than a male lion. She does not have a mane, which is the long, thick hair on a male lion's neck.

King of Beasts

There are two types of lions, African lions and Asiatic lions. A male African lion is about nine feet (2.7 m) long from nose to tail. He weighs 330 to 550 pounds (150 to 250 kilograms).

Asiatic lions are usually smaller than their African cousins. A male Asiatic lion weighs 350 to 420 pounds (160 to 190 kg).

African or Asiatic Lion?

- A male African lion has a long, thick mane that partly hides his ears.

- A male Asiatic lion has a shorter mane, and his ears can be seen clearly.

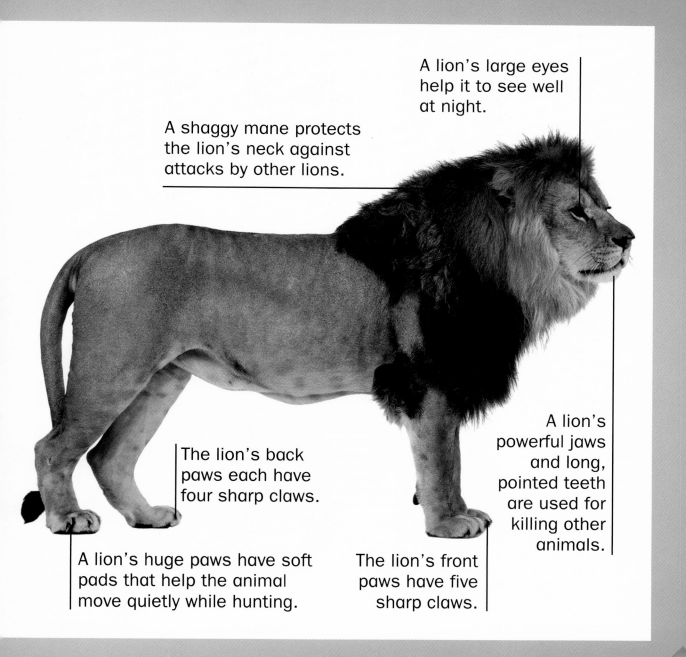

A lion's large eyes help it to see well at night.

A shaggy mane protects the lion's neck against attacks by other lions.

A lion's powerful jaws and long, pointed teeth are used for killing other animals.

The lion's back paws each have four sharp claws.

A lion's huge paws have soft pads that help the animal move quietly while hunting.

The lion's front paws have five sharp claws.

Where Do Lions Live?

Nearly all lions living in nature are found in Africa. Asiatic lions have almost died out in nature. They live only in a small part of India called the Gir Forest.

▼ Lions usually rest for 18 to 20 hours a day.

Most African lions live on the **savanna**, or grasslands, of Africa. This is their **habitat**. Here, lions hunt animals such as zebras and antelopes.

Useful Websites

www.asiatic-lion.org

Visit this website to find photographs and information about Asiatic lions.

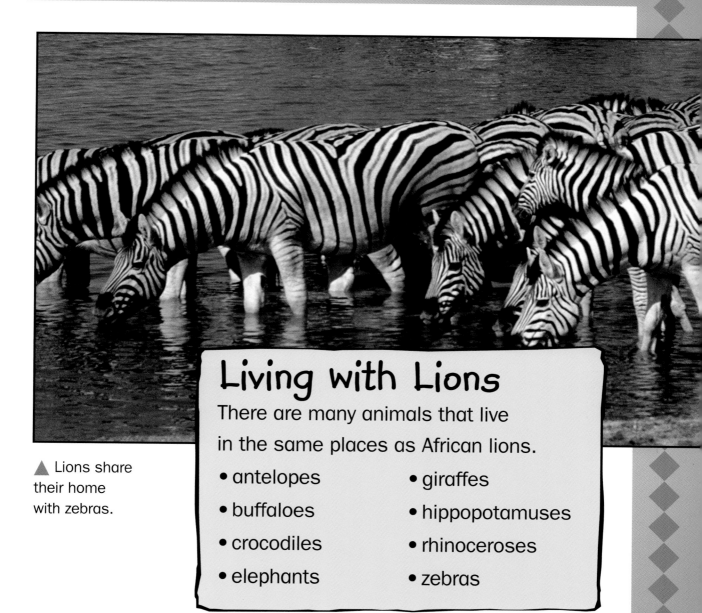

▲ Lions share their home with zebras.

Living with Lions

There are many animals that live in the same places as African lions.

- antelopes
- buffaloes
- crocodiles
- elephants
- giraffes
- hippopotamuses
- rhinoceroses
- zebras

What Do Lions Eat?

Lions are meat eaters. They need to eat at least 11 pounds (5 kg) of meat each day. Some of their favorite foods are zebras and giraffes.

A lion can run at 35 miles (56 kilometers) per hour. This is not as fast as many of the animals it hunts. So how does a lion catch food? It creeps toward its **prey** slowly and quietly. Then, it crouches in the grass and suddenly pounces.

▼ Lionesses do most of the hunting for the family.

The Lion's Lunch

- A lion may eat 70 pounds (32 kg) of meat in one meal. That is the same as eating 280 large hamburgers.

- Lionesses do most of the hunting, but the male lions eat first.

- An animal the size of a zebra can feed an entire family of lions.

- When food is difficult to find, lions can survive by eating birds, fish, insects, snakes, and even ostrich eggs.

Family Life

Lions live in family groups called **prides**. A pride is made up of lionesses and their young, and one or more male lions. The lionesses in a pride are all related. There are usually about 15 lions in a pride.

Each pride has its own home area. This area has all the food and water the pride needs to survive.

▶ A male lion will stay near his partner during mating season.

Lion Talk

- A roar can be heard from 5 miles (8 km) away.

- When a lion roars to other members of the pride, he is saying, "I am here. Where are you?"

- A roar heard by lions who are not part of the pride means, "This land is mine. Go away!"

▲ Lionesses usually stay in the same place all their lives.

Growing Up

Young lions are called cubs. For the first few weeks, newborn cubs stay hidden in a cozy **den**. Their mother feeds them and protects them from hungry predators such as leopards and hyenas.

When the cubs are four to six weeks old, they are big enough to run and play outside. They stay with their mother until they are two years old.

▶ Lion cubs start to hunt small animals when they are about 15 months old.

Useful Websites

www.lionsafari.com

Visit this website to learn more about African lions.

Comparing Weights

Human	**Lion**	

At birth	8 pounds (3.6 kg)
	2 to 4.5 pounds (1–2 kg)
At 15 months	28 pounds (12.7 kg)
	100 pounds (45 kg)
Adult male	168 pounds (76.3 kg)
	500 pounds (227 kg)

0   100   200   300   400   500 pounds

▼ A lioness protects her young until the cubs are old enough to look after themselves.

Enemies

Lions are the strongest hunters on the African savanna. They do not have many enemies, but sometimes lions fight each other for food.

Sometimes, large groups of hyenas attack lions. They will not usually approach a male lion, but they may attack a group of females. Hyenas will kill lions for food if they are able.

▶ A male lion guards his pride against enemies.

Picking a Fight

- Lions mainly fight with each other.
- Cubs fight over their mother's milk.
- Adults fight for a fair share of meat after a kill.
- Male lions attack other males who try to take over the pride.

▼ A lioness chases other females away if they come too close.

Under Threat

Humans are lions' worst enemies. People have destroyed lions' habitats by building on them or turning them into farmland. In the past, many lions were killed by people shooting them for sport.

▼ Tourists travel to Africa to see lions living in nature.

Today, people still hunt lions in some African countries. They must have a **license** to do this. Lions in Africa are now protected in national parks and wildlife reserves.

Useful Websites

www.lionresearch.org

Visit this website to read all about lions, where they live, and how to protect them.

▲ Today, the only way to see an Asiatic lion is to visit a zoo where they are kept.

Protecting the Asiatic Lion

- There are only a few Asiatic lions left in nature. They live in the Gir Forest in India.

- About 200 Asiatic lions live in zoos in North America and Europe. Zoos help protect the Asiatic lion from disappearing.

Myths and Legends

People have always seen the lion as the king of all beasts. Since early times, people around the world have told stories about lions.

In Africa and India, people worship lions as gods. In China, a Lion Dance is performed at New Year celebrations to bring good luck and happiness.

▶ Stone statues of lions guard many public buildings in China, such as city halls.

Life after Death

In Africa, some people believe that chiefs of Aboriginal groups are reborn as lions when they die.

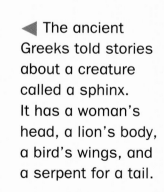

◀ The ancient Greeks told stories about a creature called a sphinx. It has a woman's head, a lion's body, a bird's wings, and a serpent for a tail.

Quiz

1. Which animals may attack lions?
(a) **giraffes** (b) **hyenas** (c) **zebras**

2. Why does a male lion have a mane?
(a) **to keep his neck warm** (b) **to hide his ears**
(c) **to protect his neck**

3. Which animals live in the same places as lions?
(a) **bears** (b) **camels** (c) **elephants**

4. What is a family group of lions called?
(a) **a pride** (b) **a habitat** (c) **a herd**

5. Up to what age does a young lion stay with its mother?
(a) **two weeks** (b) **two months** (c) **two years**

Answers:
1. (b) Hyenas may attack lions.
2. (c) A male lion has a mane to protect his neck.
3. (c) Elephants live in the same places as lions.
4. (a) A family group of lions is called a pride.
5. (c) A young lion stays with its mother until it is two years old.

Find out More

To find out more about lions, visit the websites in this book. You can also write to these organizations.

World Wildlife Fund
1250 24th Street NW
Washington, DC 20037

African Wildlife Foundation
Suite 120
1400 16th Street NW
Washington, DC 20036

Words to Know

den
an animal's home, where it may find shelter or look after its babies

habitat
the place where an animal usually lives

license
a permit to do something

mammals
animals that have hair or fur and feed milk to their young

predators
animals that hunt other animals for food

prey
an animal that is hunted for food

prides
family groups of lions

savanna
the grasslands of Africa

Index